God's People at Worship

People

The work of worship co-ordinators, worship leaders and consultations on worship

John S Lampard

Jointly published by
Division of Education and Youth
and
Methodist Publishing House

First published January 1991

ISBN 7192 0177 2
ISBN 0 946550 57 3

Illustrations: Helen Mahood

Jointly published by
Methodist Church Division of Education and Youth
2 Chester House, Pages Lane, London N10 1PR
and
Methodist Publishing House
20 Ivatt Way, Peterborough PE3 7PS

Printed by

Clifford Frost Limited, Lyon Road,
Windsor Avenue, SW19 2SE

God's People at Worship

An introduction to the series

'*God's People at Worship*' is a series of booklets about Christian worship, particularly as it takes place when all ages are present.

For simplicity, the phrase *all-age worship* is used throughout the series, despite its shortcomings. The word *worship* should need no qualification. In worship, people offer themselves – with all their similarities and differences (including their ages) – to God. Unfortunately, *worship* has come to be seen as a mainly adult activity. To describe it as *all-age* provides a useful reminder that it is the business of the whole people of God.

The booklets in the series deal with different aspects of all-age worship. In general, the emphasis is practical, looking at *How?* questions. However, *Why?* questions are also dealt with, particularly in the introductory volume, *One*.

'*God's People at Worship*' is for worship leaders; for those who plan, prepare and co-ordinate worship in local churches; for workers with children and young people; for church musicians; for people who are creative in written or spoken word, dance, drama or visual arts; for stewards, members of worship consultations and Church Councils and all those who make decisions about the church's worship. But, above all, our hope is that these booklets will be read and used by Christian people of all ages who care about worship.

The current volume, *People*, explores the role of those with a special responsibility for worship within the local church, especially worship co-ordinators, worship leaders and consultations on worship.

'*God's People at Worship*' is produced jointly by the Methodist Publishing House and the Division of Education and Youth, in consultation with representatives of the Division of Ministries and the Worship Commission.

The General Editor of the series is Rev. David Gamble, working with an Advisory Group (Mrs Judy Jarvis, Rev. John Lampard, Mr Brian Sharp and Mr Brian Thornton).

Contents

Acknowledgements

Parts of this booklet are the product of a working party which produced an (unpublished) report in 1987 which dealt with the themes in this booklet. The contributions of the following members are gratefully acknowledged:

Terry Ayres, Ellen Barber, Maureen Edwards, Geoffrey Morris, David Palmer, Alan Saunders, Jeffrey Smith and Wilf Tooley. The report of the working party was presented to members of the commission on worship. This booklet expands on some of the issues raised in the report '*Let the people worship*'.

1 What's happening?

Exciting, unusual, new, stimulating and for a few people threatening, things are happening in *some* churches in *some* Circuits. Worship which is live, vital and truly evangelical (in that it is *good news*) is taking place. This new approach to worship fits no simple pattern or style. It can be traditional, charismatic, formal or spontaneous. By its very nature it does not fit into categories.

Its marks include:

- Concern for all ages at worship
- Growth in congregations
- Widespread participation
- Preparation for worship by groups
- Joy and thankfulness
- A linking of learning and worship
- Planning by preachers and congregations
- The development of worship co-ordinators.

This development, which is admittedly patchy throughout the country, represents a significant growth and development in worship and is one that can usefully be explored in other churches and circuits.

This new pattern of worship does raise deep and radical questions about:

- The nature of authority in worship
- The role of the Superintendent Minister in plan-making
- The part played by local preachers and ministers
- The existence or otherwise of Circuit worship policies
- The role of consultations on worship
- Amateurism and professionalism
- How we can discern the role of the Holy Spirit.

You may be one of the readers who find parts of this booklet threatening and possibly disturbing. If it has this effect on you, you might like to ask yourself, '*Why?*' Resistance to change is equally likely to come from ministers, local preachers or local congregations. Preachers and congregations can both complain about dullness and lack of involvement of the other party or parties.

Some readers will identify in this booklet many of the things that are happening and have happened for many years in churches known to them. If this is so they might like to ask themselves, '*What are some of the implications in what we are doing?*'

Other readers, again, might ask, '*How can some of these things happen in our church or Circuit?*'

We hope there is sufficient information and guidance in this booklet to stimulate discussion, action and reflection. The questions at the end of each section are posed in order to stimulate discussion in any context where worship is discussed, such as consultations on worship, Church Family committees, Church Councils, local preachers' meetings, staff meetings, housegroups and fellowships, etc.

This booklet concentrates on the work of worship co-ordinators, worship leaders and consultations on worship. Here the people of God pray, plan and prepare for the worship of all the people of God. That is why it is called *People*.

2 Changes in worship

Because the activity of worship is always changing, it is sometimes difficult to appreciate the extent of the changes that have taken place over the last twenty years or so. The following account, by a minister, describes his conversion from a traditional formal pattern to a new and more lively style.

A minister's experience

As a teenager I grew up in a church which used the Authorised Version of the Bible, the old *Methodist Hymn Book* and a very predictable, rambling hymn-sandwich form of worship. The great innovation of the time was the Family Service, but this hardly disturbed the general pattern of worship except that it involved a longer children's address and a slightly shorter sermon, intended to be more simple. Children did not appear at Communion.

When I began my ministry, the *New English Bible* had arrived and though *You* rather than *Thou* found its way into my prayers, it was only just acceptable.

Visual aids were beginning to have some prominence, and any self-respecting church would have its Family Service. The children were beginning to take a more prominent part. I was by no means certain in my mind that the Family Service was as good as the '*real worship*' with its full sermon that took place on other occasions - but it had the advantage

that more people came, and they seemed to value the pattern of worship.

The new services began to arrive with their more practical, modern and less wordy approach. The mould of worship was showing distinct signs of cracking. I began to have interview services in which I would invite members of the congregation to tell me about their work for Christ in the community and invite others from outside the local church to tell their story.

An Open University degree course enabled me to see how the Church had undergone a tremendous adaptation due to its contact with the world through its mission. I also began to see more clearly the Old Testament roots. I realized the possibility of adapting the Jewish *Seder*, or Passover, into an Easter *Seder* – the telling of the Easter Story around a table with symbols and readings, perhaps in the homes of members rather than in the church.

Family Services were developing a link with *Partners in Learning*, and we experimented with W E B (Worship, Education and Breakfast). The visual aid was a montage showing photographs of people from the congregation. Sunday School leaders would take the *Partners in Learning* theme and introduce each part of the Sunday School into the worship to do something quite specific in line with the service theme. Playlets, *Partners in Praise,* posters and dramatic readings found their way into worship. It all seemed so necessary if the church was to adapt to the real world in which it is set. Children stayed in church and came to Communion, coming to the rail for a blessing. A new service was written to cut out repetition and enable the service to flow from one element to another so that the whole congregation knew where it was going in the service. It was ninety per cent the old service, but re-ordered to make it more intelligible to an all-age worship congregation. It was a remarkable success.

The need for a team of people to put together special services was now well established. A new hymn was written and an Easter Symbol Service put together with all sorts of preparation in which parents and children could engage. The service came with all the necessary instructions including how to bake the special large buns that needed to be displayed. Painted egg designs were invented and recommended. Prayers were written and the themes established together with a special commitment of a gift to the National Children's Home.

In this environment, churches in the Circuit became full of inventiveness and were beginning to include dance in their worship.

We even built a whole service based on dance-mime. The imagination was now free to praise God. Children started to come to Communion not only for a blessing but sometimes to take the elements themselves when the theme of the service was one of the aspects of God's all-embracing grace. Video was used as the basis of discussion and illustration within worship. Locally written hymns, poetry, dance, testimony, music groups, visual aids (including a Bible-sized Ark of the Covenant), written prayers, flower arrangements, sketches - all these were finding their way into worship.

I am no longer able to say that these things are gimmicks or to count the services in which they play a part as less *'real'* than the traditional services. The blessings received have been tremendous, and some of our worship has hit the local headlines. God is in this thing and he is calling many to join in to see him afresh in worship.

Questions for discussion

1 Can you identify the major changes that have taken place in worship in your church?

2 From where did the pressure for change come?

3 What have been the major disadvantages/advantages of the changes?

4 What further changes would you like to see?

This is one minister's experience. It stems from a concern that people may be allowed to be responsible for their worship. The days of Rev. or Mr *'Do-it-all-myself'* are slowly being numbered.

How can we liberate people to *'Let the people worship?'*

People within the church must act. The next two sections look at the very different roles of the worship co-ordinator and the worship leader.

3 Worship co-ordinators

A visiting preacher received the following letter about a month before she was planning to take a service.

> We look forward to welcoming you to our church on *14 June*. The congregation like to share in worship with you and I am pleased to offer the following resources which you may wish to use when planning the service.
>
> We have a music group, a choral reading group, a singing group, a drama group and several individual musicians. We also have a cassette recorder and overhead projector. Individual members are happy to read Bible passages. If any of these can assist you, please let me know. If you can guide us on the theme of your worship it will assist us in our preparation.

Under the signature of the writer were the words *'Worship co-ordinator'*.

A number of churches are now appointing worship co-ordinators to perform two roles:

a to liaise with visiting preachers so that the varied resources in the local church can be offered for use in worship;

b to co-ordinate and develop the talents for worship participation which already exist in the local church.

a Liaison with visiting preachers.

Visiting preachers often feel inhibited from asking for contributions and assistance from a local church. *Whom should they contact? Can the church supply the resources? Who will make the arrangements? Is there a plug handy for a cassette recorder? What about an overhead projector?* In some situations church stewards might be able to help with this. The appointment of a worship co-ordinator, who makes contact with the visiting preacher in advance of the service (if only to say what *cannot* be offered – such as the dramatization of the fall of Jerusalem) will assist the preparation of the act of worship. (Whether contact is made by preacher or Worship Co-ordinator, the importance of adequate warning cannot be over emphasized.)

A worship co-ordinator should not be thought of only in terms of all-age worship, although this is the context in which many have arisen.

A London church (Wakefield Street in the Newham circuit) produced a worship resources list which offers to visiting preachers an enticing and attractive list of resource people and facilities. It includes

- details of *hymns and song books* available,
- details of the *public address system* (including how *records* and *cassette tapes* can be played,
- *equipment* (overhead projector, slide projector and slide sets etc);
- *resource people* including actors, dialogue readers, artists (one of whom does not want to draw people!), a dozen dancers, thirty-two musicians, thirty-three singers and five writers.

Such talent should tax the most creative minister or local preacher. About forty people participate in worship groups which re-form every quarter, so members get used to working with different people. Almost all of the circuit staff and all the local preachers work with one of the teams. The system has, incidentally, produced at least five new local preachers. It is also significant that the worship team can draw on the willing help of people who do not normally attend the church. It thus fulfils an evangelical task.

b Co-ordinating local talent

If a local congregation is to offer even a few of these worship resources, it will be necessary to seek them out, develop, train and co-ordinate them. The worship co-ordinator thus has a creative and administrative role. Traditionally, churches have not been good at seeking out musical and other skills among their members. Young people often have talents which are ignored. In some circumstances they can accompany hymns. In a small church a clarinet or flute can be a refreshing change.

Music can accompany the offering or during a meditation.

Some local churches can put together a small orchestra or choir. The worship co-ordinator may not do all this herself, but may organise other people to do it.

A worship co-ordinator can encourage people to read lessons or take other parts in worship. If members of a congregation feel that what they can offer is being valued, they will not only attend more regularly, but they will feel that an act of worship gives them value – an important theological understanding about our humanity. We value God in worship and God values us.

Questions

1 Has your church thought of appointing a worship co-ordinator?

2 What are the latent or hidden resources in your congregation or community which a co-ordinator could marshall for contributions to worship?

3 Would the appointment of a worship co-ordinator and team pose a threat to leaders of traditional patterns of worship? How could this be dealt with?

4 Worship leaders

There is some evidence, from different parts of the country, that a few people are feeling a call to be worship leaders rather than local preachers. Their sense of call is to an integrative ministry in worship. Perhaps they correspond to the American pattern of liturgists, who are responsible for the planning of an act of worship and its leadership, apart from the sermon itself.

Obviously, many ministers and local preachers would not like the idea of losing responsibility for a major part of an act of worship. This does not mean that they cannot and should not work with someone who has studied and trained in worship leadership skills.

A worship leader might link with a minister, local preacher or the worship co-ordinator in planning and sharing in the leadership of an act of worship. In some instances, the same person may be co-ordinator in the way described in the previous section and leader, but the skills are distinctly different.

It has been said that every minister (and we assume the same of local preachers) has a natural bent towards being either a leader of worship or a preacher. Those who lean towards worship leadership see the whole act of worship as of primary importance, and will spend more time on preparing and organizing it. Such people see the sermon

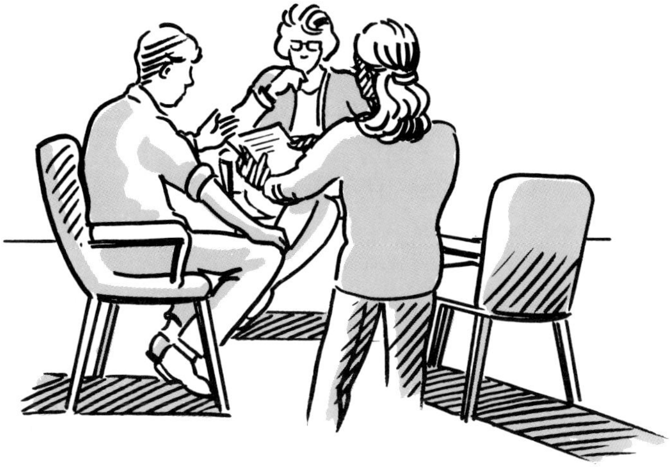

as secondary. Those in the latter category see themselves primarily as *preachers* and the rest of the service as secondary. These two categories present *ideal-types* and many who lead worship would claim to straddle both categories. However, the categories are a helpful means of analysing the primary aim and skill of those who lead worship.

Some churches have developed teams of worship leaders. At Notting Hill, in West London, when the circuit plan is made, teams of worship leaders are appointed along with the name of the preacher. The team meets with the preacher and shares in an act of co-operative preparation. Ideas for the sermon can be discussed, Bible passages studied together and responsibility shared. One of the advantages of a team approach is that new members, who may have little or no experience of leading worship or speaking in public, can join a team and at first play only a small part. As confidence and skill develops, they are expected to play a fuller part. Those who are experienced in leading worship as ministers and local preachers are sometimes humbled by the hours of careful preparation put into a small part of the act of worship by such people.

Obviously, questions about training and accreditation arise (and are dealt with in chapter 5). At a time when the Church has a policy of ending the role of unaccredited preachers such as auxiliary or helper, etc, it is hardly likely to create a new generation of non-accredited worship leaders who do not preach. We are unlikely in the foreseeable future to create a new order of fully accredited worship leaders, but the day may come. However, the creativity engendered in some worship leaders must not be lost to the worshipping life of the church.

Questions

1 Would you welcome the development of worship leaders or worship leadership teams as separate groups within the church?

2 Would such a development detract from the traditional roles of ministers and local preachers?

5 Consultations on worship

The consultation on worship was one of the fruits of Methodist restructuring in the mid-1970s. In view of the widely held perception that worship is at the heart of the Church, it is strange that it was and still is seen as a voluntary meeting. Each Church Council should ask itself, *'Do we resolve to set up a Consultation on Worship?'*

The *role* of the consultation is to 'advise the Church Council on matters related to the conduct of public worship in the Local Church'. Standing Orders envisage it as advising the Church Council on special services, but little else. This may be one of the reasons it was not the instant success its planners hoped. Its membership is set out in Standing Order 652 as follows.

652 Consultation on Worship. (1) The Consultation on Worship shall consist of:

(i) the Superintendent;

(ii) the minister, probationer, deaconess or deacon having pastoral charge of the Local Church;

(iii) any minister or probationer entitled to voting membership of the General Church Meeting by virtue of Standing Order 606 (4);

(iv) the convenor of the consultation, appointed by the Church Council;

(v) the church stewards;

(vi) the communion stewards;

(vii) the general superintendent of the Sunday-school or junior church or his or her representatives;

(viii) two class leaders or pastoral visitors, appointed by the Pastoral Committee;

(ix) the organist;

(x) the choir director;

(xi) all local preachers who are members in the Local Church;

(xii) any other local preachers in the Circuit who may be appointed to the consultation by the Church Council;

(xiii) others with appropriate qualifications, appointed by the Church Council.

The worship co-ordinator may be convenor of this consultation, but if not he or she together with worship leaders should be members of the consultation.

In 1977, the Local Preachers' Committee in the Division of Ministries prepared the following guidelines for worship consultations. They offer suggestions for an agenda, although no one meeting would wish to go through all the following points.

Guidelines for consultations on worship

1 *Preparatory matters*

a It may prove helpful if the initial session of the *Worship Consultation*, or a prior meeting of the whole congregation, is an informal social occasion with refreshments.

b The *constitutional position* should be noted.

Standing Order 652 gives the list of those entitled to attend a worship consultation, and describes its function as follows:

> The consultation shall advise the Church Council on matters related to the conduct of public worship in the Local Church.

(Notice also that there is a question on the agenda of the Church Family Committee: '*What is the report of the Consultation on Worship? Where there is no Consultation on Worship what have we to say about the conduct of public worship?'*) There is a question on the agenda of the Local Preachers' Meeting: *'Communications from Church Family Committees or Church Councils concerning the conduct of worship*'.

It is necessary to see that the lines of communication with the local preachers' meeting (both ways!) are in good working order.

c No formal agenda or minutes may be necessary, but a memorandum may prove a useful link between meetings.

d Full lay participation should be encouraged.

2 *Subjects for discussion at the worship consultation*

a *What is worship?*

Is it for the glory of God? Or the inspiration of people? What are its bare essentials? What, then, ought to be our priorities in worship?

b *How can we make the best use of Sunday?*

Should morning and evening services be similar? Are our Junior Church leaders able to hear sermons and come to Communion? Can any of our training work be done on Sundays? Can we meet informally as well as for worship?

c *Use of ministers and local preachers - the circuit plan.*

Is there opportunity for ministers and local preachers - and other lay people for that matter - to *team up* in the conduct of worship and preaching?

d *Lay participation in services*

(reading of lessons, intercessory prayers, the use of groups and fellowships in the preparation of services and sermons).
How can we persuade people that the service is their service?

e *Family Worship and Parade Services*

The use of the Lectionary and *Partners in Learning* (or whatever scheme may be used in its place).

f *The Methodist Service Book*
Ought we not to spend one session of the Worship Consultation going through *The Sunday Service*, *The Sunday Service without the Lord's Supper* and the

Appendices (pp B5-B39), and ask how they could be used to enrich our worship?

g *Baptism*

Is this sacrament given a prominent place in the worship of the people?

h *The Lord's Supper*

Do we make this the joyful celebration it is meant to be? Does it stand in its own right or is it *tacked on* to another service? Do lay people share in the conduct of it?

i *The festivals and other special services*

Are the great festivals of Christmas, Easter and Pentecost given pride of place in the annual cycle of our worship? Can we introduce new worship material into them?

j *Hymns and songs for worship. Music*

Is there any musical talent, instrumental or vocal, that we are not using?

k *New forms of worship*

Role play, interviews, visuals, etc.
If these are not overdone, can they make our worship more lively and stimulating? Are we allowing space and time for spontaneity in our services?

l *Forms of preaching*

Would team preaching (several people conducting worship and preaching *together* in one place; they may visit any place once, or more than once, but always go together; they are a team) or planned preaching (several people conducting worship *separately* in one place, or several places, usually in succession; their services and sermons are linked by the subject matter) be of use to us? Or some combination of the two?

m *Feed-back*

How can we best discover the reaction of our people to changes in worship and preaching? To what extent should we consult them?

n *Ecumenical dimensions of worship*

Do we exploit to the full the opportunities afforded by the present ecumenical situation?

These words of advice and encouragement from 1977 have stood the test of time and offer a valuable agenda for the worship consultation.

The next section sets out the way in which a consultation on worship has developed in a creative way and produced a worship advisory group and a worship group.

First steps of a consultation on worship

Our consultation on worship is a vigorous infant. It is just over four years old, but has already held five meetings. Normally about twelve to fifteen of us attend and the ground covered has included:

1 *Discussion of fundamentals*

We wrestled with questions like, '*What is worship?*', '*Why is it important?*' and '*How can our worship be improved?*' We have not discovered the final answers yet, but we have grown together as a group as we have tackled these topics.

2 *Discussion of themes*

Several times we have taken up themes which could cause misunderstanding or contention, such as *children and Communion*, or *the use of music in worship*. Our differences remain, but we have a forum where new and old items can be discussed with charity and (sometimes) humour.

3 *Arrangements for special services*

At our meetings, we have looked back at recent special services (Junior Church Anniversary; the Carol Concert) to rejoice in the good points and learn from our mistakes. We also look forward to coming events, perhaps identifying smaller groups to carry out detailed planning.

4 *The Study course*

To provide pegs for our thinking, we decided that as a group we would tackle the Study Course on *all-age worship* published by the Division of Ministries, devoting the first half of each meeting to a brief talk and discussion led by one of our members. Our discussions have been enlivened, in particular, by the contributions of one member who has seen American Methodism in action and been impressed by their provision of Christian Education and Worship for all age-groups on a Sunday morning. The talking continues!

Our motto seems to have become *Unity in Diversity*, which sounds like a recipe for health and growth in the local church.

All this might look fairly formal and traditional, but the consultation on worship can be the means through which exciting and more radical things can happen in worship. Of course, a deadly dull, complacent congregation, wedded to dreary traditionalism is unlikely to be set on fire by new ideas or to want to be, and we can suggest no solution to such a problem. We believe and hope that such congregations are a minority, and that what is offered here can excite and stimulate many potentially vital congregations.

In addition to the questions raised in the 1977 Guidelines, a consultation on worship might grapple with some of the following.

1 Should a visiting preacher have total control over what happens in worship? Can a congregation tell a visiting preacher what they want to do?

2 In what ways can a congregation participate?

3 What should happen if a congregation wants to do one thing and a visiting preacher something else?

4 How can worship be freed-up so that it taps the hidden resources of the congregation and does not rely unnecessarily heavily on the preacher?

In a large church, it might be appropriate for the consultation on worship to delegate some of its concerns to a worship advisory group. This is an account of such a group.

A Worship Advisory Group

The consultation on worship has appointed a small working group, *the worship advisory group*, to encourage more participation in services, on occasions when our own minister and local preacher are planned.

The group meets once or twice per quarter. The group's brief covers all-age worship, participation in family services and special occasions like Mothering Sunday, Remembrance Sunday, Good Friday, Christmas, etc. The services and occasions needing help are identified by the minister and the ideas produced are subject to his agreement, but he does not find it necessary to meet with the group.

Many of the ideas are by no means new. They include the occasional rearrangement of chairs to form a circle or semi-circle, the use of audio-visuals, religious drama, meditation, music, theme services, etc. Responsibility for parts of a service is often delegated to particular families, house-groups, Junior Church, the drama club, choir, etc, who have also contributed ideas that have been woven into acts of worship.

One valuable exercise helped to make Family Communions more interesting and less *drawn out.*

One member of the group (hidden) timed each part of the service with a stop-watch to help us see more clearly where it was likely to be tedious to some of the young people. From this information, we worked out a form of service lasting no more than fifty minutes and which includes most of the liturgy, a short address, three or four hymns and Communion for up to two hundred people served in a continuous procession by the minister and three helpers.

1 Involving other groups in the church and co-ordinating their suggestions widens the opportunities for all to participate.

2 The minister appreciates this practical help and support to make worship the offering of the whole people of God. It frees him from the stress of making detailed arrangements to concentrate on what he has to offer.

3 Over the last five or six years many members, who would not normally think they had anything to say in public, have been enabled to make a significant contribution to our worship.

In a Yorkshire village church a worship group has been in existence for over fifteen years. Its role and development has been more radical than either of the last two examples.

A worship group

Background

The group has been in existence for over fifteen years, but has increased in size and scope as the church membership has increased from fifty to one hundred and twenty.

Membership

The average attendance is now about a dozen, consisting of the minister (who has three other churches), six or seven local preachers, representatives from the Sunday School and miscellaneous co-options to span ages and interests.

The role

Consultation

a review and evaluation of services in the past quarter is undertaken, and suggestions made for the future.

Preparation

decisions are taken on which Sunday the services, including a series of services such as Advent and Lent, should be undertaken by the worship group, and appropriate themes and study material agreed on.

Leadership

the leaders, ministerial and lay, are agreed for each of the selected services.

Co-operation

names are suggested for the named leaders to be involved in the preparation and conduct of worship.

Invitations

approaches are made to visitors, both ministerial and lay, from other churches and denominations both to lead and to participate in some of the worship group services, and congregational involvement is offered to visitors.

Authority in relation to the circuit plan

The plan

Each service undertaken by the worship group appears on the plan as WG If the leader of worship is either a minister or a local preacher, the name of the person appears on the plan, so as to avoid duplication.

Authority

The Superintendent Minister and the circuit local preachers' meeting accept the work and authority of the worship group because its services are prepared in the context of consultation with the church's own minister and local preachers.

Accreditation

Occasionally, the worship group agrees to nominate a non-accredited person to lead worship, e.g. Sunday School teacher, local headmaster, religious education lecturer/advisor, but in such cases the minister or a local preacher liaises with the person concerned on behalf of the worship group.

Exceptionally, non-qualified persons are nominated to take a service, e.g. the young wives' group for Mothering Sunday. In this instance, an accredited preacher will take responsibility for the service and offer advice and assistance in preparation and training, even though such a person may not actively participate in the actual conduct of worship.

Presentation

Many worship group services follow a traditional form, but when the leaders are non-accredited, short addresses or dramatic presentation may take the place of a formal sermon.

Most worship group services, especially at morning worship, actively involve children in the leadership, e.g. offering of the opening prayer, announcing hymns, reading a lesson.

All worship group services include participation by members of the congregation. This includes readings, prayers, song, etc.

Conclusions

- Worship group services are better attended than an average non-worship group service.
- Members of the congregation have been helped by listening to the words and thoughts of a friend or neighbour, and have felt more closely identified with the leader and the leadership of worship.
- These services have often had a greater relevance for the congregation because they have been planned to meet a specific need or are led by people who are more aware of the life and needs of the congregation.
- We have been able to provide continuity of thought and theme; this has had a particular value at periods such as Lent when the Sunday service can serve to introduce housegroup themes.
- Those who have led worship have found it a rewarding experience and a means of developing and deepening their Christian life.
- A few who have led worship have subsequently felt the call to offer themselves formally to train as local preachers.
- We have had the opportunity to experiment with forms of worship which attempt to relate to the modern world of mass communication and education.
- Above all else, we have tried to make our people recognise their value and worth, from the youngest to the oldest. We truly seek to be ONE in CHRIST.

Questions

1 Does your church have a consultation on worship?

2 If so, what does it do? If not, should one be formed?

3 What do you think of the ideas put forward in this section?

6 The generation gap

All who are concerned in the leadership of worship are aware of the different hopes and expectations of the different generations present in an act of worship. The following is a heartfelt plea by an older person who longs to see worship which speaks to the hearts and minds of younger people. No easy solutions are offered, but some indication of the directions in which congregations can move are shared.

Going to church

Very few young people today just 'go to church'. To follow in parents' footsteps for the sake of tradition/habit as a Sunday activity is out of the question. Many leisure activities are now available, transport is easier. TV in the home, pressure of school, study and homework often eat into the weekend. Mum often works all week, and the weekends are busy for her as well.

I believe that to hold our young people, we must show in worship a Living Lord and a Living Response. We need to show Jesus alive in our lives, approach, outlook, behaviour in church, home, world, community. There must be joy and wonder in our worship.

Challenge to young people

Young people respond to challenge. Many of them want to know what the Bible says about social evils, moral issues. Relevant discussion and teaching of standards are readily listened to. The fear of nuclear and chemical warfare is real. Personal experience and honesty is welcomed.

What is expected of the Christian in terms of commitment and behaviour? How do they cope with demands made on them by friends, peer groups and families not in sympathy with church life? What is heaven, is there a hell, what is the devil, is the occult really dangerous? They latch on to the great promises of God. Good clear-cut teaching is very important.

Many young people enjoy pop music and sport, they have their heroes.

They latch on to CND, Greenpeace and politics. They will hang their hats on to one peg or another. When they find it, it is with enthusiasm and they promote it. Let us make sure our *peg* is there fair and square and that our churches offer a place to which they can invite their friends.

Visual worship

So much teaching today is visual. Pictures accompany television news. To listen to long, complicated or involved sermons is felt to be unbearable. They will not come. They loathe being *talked down to* and find it quite embarrassing. Visual aids are important to them, there are many resources to call on; posters, banners and pictures all play a part in using the eyes.

Drama or movement worked out in the context of a Bible passage or song is very beneficial. Worshippers have to stop and think about every sentence and express it using their bodies. It can be a very healthy part of our worship pattern.

Words and music

Music plays a tremendous part in the lives of young people. They are plugged in as they walk around, travel and eat! They have music centres in their rooms and the words of popular music become background to daily life. For the young Christian, the whole concept of song is of paramount importance. They like to express it by clapping and raising hands. Let us embed the words of truth in their hearts and minds by offering the scope for them.

Relevant worship

And so I could go on . . . In the light of all this, what can we do to encourage our young people to embark on a worship pattern that is helpful and relevant?

They are not interested in gimmicks, and we must avoid *concert worship*. A feeling of warmth and love embracing all must be felt. Worship must engage the whole self, the whole church family. Worship must have an excitement and anticipation in which, we all share, knowing that God delights in us and our worship gives us pleasure – a two-way enjoyment. Worship is for God's benefit – not just ours; let us get away from the *one man show* by the person appointed to preach. We ALL have input we can share. Even if the preacher is seen to be doing all the apparent leading, our measure of giving is felt.

We must aim at participation, this creates interest and variety. We must use all the senses, find new freedom of expression, new music, dance, drama, all at various levels and times as appropriate.
Let everything that has breath, praise the Lord! This idea really engages young people today. It is important to remind them that God revealed himself in Jesus Christ, the greatness, power, majesty, the awe, the holiness, the love, etc. Worship helps to provide a setting to focus minds on the wonder of it all, allowing God to act through the power of the Holy Spirit.

Prayers must be meaningful and concise. Special needs and concerns of the local congregations must be made known. Up-to-date national and world affairs should be mentioned, things that really relate.

A balance of the old and the new is very important. Our traditional hymns can be as relevant now as when written. They are fundamental to our faith, youngsters relate to and love some of them. Modern worship songs embrace scripture in song and this is a way of learning the Word. More new music books are being published than ever before. Many go to Spring Harvest and other similar events. They latch on to the songs especially published for these occasions. Most churches in this area attracting young folk have *Mission Praise*, and *Junior Praise* is now taking off.

Let us get away from two sections, Junior Church and Adult Church. We are all one, but the transition from Junior to Adult Church can be a real culture shock, sometimes the point at which we lose those we nurture. Howard Mellor, in his book on family worship, writes 'Worship is as many sided as a diamond, as we turn it we see a new face and aspect that helps us appreciate the diamond as a whole'. In our Methodist system we have many lay people leading our services, particularly in country churches. We need to be alert in our fellowships, watching for the gifts and the potential of our people moulding it all into all our acts of worship. Let us draw out the gifts they didn't realise they had. Let us create the seed-bed for growth and an understanding of what the Holy Spirit can do when we release ourselves to be used of Him. All the facets and the variety of many diamonds lie dormant in a great many of our churches.

Questions

1 Has your church enquired of the young people their views on Sunday worship?

2 Why is it that many youngsters seem able to relate to Junior Church or Sunday School, but seem unable to relate to Sunday worship?

3 If one answer to question 2 above is that children have opportunity to express themselves more in Junior Church than in church worship, how can we offer further opportunities for expression in our Sunday worship?

7 People centred worship

Participation in worship is a much-used phrase, and is resisted, rightly, by some who say it is just about more and more people doing something in worship. We need to move beyond *participation* to a deep understanding of what it is to lead worship in such a way that all who share in the service *own* it for themselves by their personal involvement in the act of worship.

Congregation centred worship

All leaders of worship must think deeply and hard about the manner in which they lead worship, if members of the congregation are to feel involved in what is happening.

Participation in the 1990s

Participation has become much more prevalent in a number of walks of life in the last twenty years. Television companies encourage it (quiz games, a variety of 'Any Questions' type programmes, and a big increase in participatory fun-programmes). National and local radio channels all have 'phone-ins, and encourage participation enthusiastically.

Politicians have surgeries, schools have pupil-councils, governing bodies have parents – all of us can influence thinking if we wish. Hence, so the current very telling phrase goes, we come to *own* the decision. Viewers and listeners *own* the programme they participate in and therefore hold very different views from those who are passive listeners!

The individual

Because each member of the congregation is thus vitally important, a very careful thinking through of the nature of involvement in worship is needed. An analogy from some current thinking in education offers helpful insights.

Pupil-centred learning

For the best teachers, pupils have always been central to the learning process. In the last twenty years, however, many more teachers have taken to emphasizing the role young people play in their *own* learning. The thinking, considerably simplified, argues:

- that the child is central to the learning process;
- that the child has rights;
- that by placing the child centrally, the benefits to the child are very considerable.

There are many more points the protagonists of child-centred teaching would make, but they are not relevant at this point. All that we need to draw from the argument is that teachers committed to this philosophy place children right in the middle of their thinking, thus bestowing on them responsibilities and possibilities.

Two of the basic assumptions made by Donna Brandes and Paul Ginnis in their book *A guide to student-centred learning* (Basil Blackwell 1986) are:

a the person has a willingness to change and grow, indeed a need and desire to do so, and at the same time (s)he has resistance and fear about changing; these two factors are equally acceptable

b the person is in charge of him/herself, is fully responsible for his/her behaviour, can participate or not, as (s)he chooses.

What does all this have to say about involvement in worship?

The main conclusion is that we should be considering what *congregation-centred leadership of worship* is about. In understanding this, a number of important points should be borne in mind.

a Of course God is the focal point (the only point) of worship. However, there is more to it than that! The task of all leaders of worship is to act as facilitators, to help members of the congregation to worship God.

b If we replace the word *child* by the word *congregation* in the section headed *pupil-centred learning* (above), the significance of participation is strengthened.

c Members of the congregation need to participate in the act of worship. At one (very important) level, that means doing readings, leading prayers, taking part in drama, mime, etc. (The inclusion of other people should never mean reduction in standards, by the way!)
At another level, involvement is much more complex and refers to that relationship between worship leader and congregation whereby members of the congregation feel that they *really* are positively taking part in the service. Some styles of Methodist leadership have just this effect; others do not. The minister or local preacher needs to lead worship in a way that is open and warm,

even friendly: that is actually enabling the Holy Spirit to work - i.e., drawing out worship from the participant.

d Modern teaching methods - now epitomized in GCSE - assert that children are not mere vessels to fill with knowledge. Teachers should not just attempt to impose a method on them and fill them with facts. Similarly, leaders of worship should not impose a filling process - rather, they should be drawing from people their worship and bringing together all this activity into an offering for God.

e In good teaching in schools, story-telling is considered very important. The story needs to be told in such a way that the children *own* the story afterwards - that is, it is theirs. It is theirs to respond to and it is theirs as a basis for further thought or action. We need to lead worship so that it ceases to be ours, as leaders, but becomes *owned* by the members of the congregation, so that they can respond to God.

Conclusion

We must not look just for individualistic, gifted leaders of worship, rather men and women who can communicate a warmth to the congregation so that all wish to worship God, and all are certain that somehow they are involved in the offering of worship to God.

Questions

1 What involvement in worship is necessary before Sunday Worship takes place? e.g. preparation of heart and mind; prayer; communication of a sense of expectancy.

2 How can the idea of *people-centred worship* be developed?

Recent years have seen increased interest and involvement in the planning, preparation and leadership of worship by members of local congregations. Worship is, after all, the business of the whole people of God.

People looks at the work of worship coordinators, worship leaders and consultations on worship and offers new ways for members of local congregations to 'own' their worship.

John Lampard is a Methodist minister and is currently the Local Preachers' Secretary at the Division of Ministries of the Methodist Church.